Take Control of Trading

Paige Beckham

Paige Beckham

Paige Beckham

Legal and legal data
Copyright holder: © Sebastian MG
Author: © Paige Beckham
Year: 2024

This book, including its content and design, is protected by copyright © laws. No part of this work may be reproduced, distributed, or transmitted in any form or by any means, without the prior written permission of the author, except in cases provided by law.

First edition
All rights reserved

Paige Beckham

Index

Introduction to Emotional Trading	7
Trader Psychology	10
The Impact of Emotions on Trading Decisions	14
The Importance of Emotional Control	18
Identification of Emotions	22
Strategies to Reduce Emotional Influence	25
Mindfulness and Trading	29
Techniques of breathing and relaxation	33
Developing an Emotionally Resilient Trading Plan	37
Maintain Discipline in Emotional Situations	41
Learning from Emotional Losses	45
Mentoring and Psychological Support in Trading	49
Strategies to Recover from Large Losses	53
Emotional Simulation Exercises	57
Post-Trade Analysis from an Emotional Perspective	61
Community and Support among Traders	65
Continuous Review and Adjustment of the Emotional Control Plan	69
Maintaining Emotional Balance in the Long Term	73

Paige Beckham

Paige Beckham

Introduction to Emotional Trading

Trading is more than simply buying and selling financial assets. At the heart of every trading decision there are human emotions at play. Imagine this scenario: you're in front of your screen, watching the graphics change rapidly. Suddenly, the price rises more than expected and you feel a wave of excitement and enthusiasm. Should you buy more? Or should you sell before the market turns against you?

These decisions may be influenced by your emotions at the time. Emotional trading refers to how our emotions, such as fear, greed, euphoria or panic, can affect our financial decisions. Surprisingly, even the most experienced traders can fall into the trap of emotions. This can lead to making impulsive decisions or ignoring a carefully laid out plan.

Why do emotions play such an important role in trading? Because we are human beings, not machines. Our emotions are intertwined with our perception of risk and reward. When the market goes up, we can feel more confident and inclined to take risks. But when the market falls, fear can lead us to sell hastily to avoid further losses.

It is important to recognize that emotional trading is not exclusive to beginners. Even traders with years of experience can be affected. The key is not to eliminate emotions (because that is impossible), but to learn to manage them effectively. This involves developing an emotional awareness of how you feel in different market situations and how those emotions can influence your decisions.

In this book, we will explore how understanding and managing your emotions can make the difference between success and failure in trading. You will learn practical strategies for staying calm under pressure, how to avoid falling into common emotional traps, and how to develop a trading plan that takes your emotional response into account.

Remember, trading is not just about numbers and charts, but also about how you manage your emotions. Get ready to explore an exciting journey towards emotional trading control!

Trader Psychology

The psychology of the trader is like the hidden engine that drives every decision in the complex world of trading. Have you ever wondered why two traders facing the same situation can react so differently? The answer lies in how our mind processes information, manages emotions and evaluates risk.

Imagine you are in front of your trading screen, watching prices fluctuate rapidly. At that moment, your brain is working at full speed, evaluating possibilities and calculating risks. But it's not just about numbers and graphs; Our decisions are also shaped by our personality, our past experiences in the market, and our future expectations.

One of the keys to understanding the psychology of the trader lies in how we respond to risk. Some traders have a natural inclination toward risk, seeking out opportunities that promise big profits despite potential dangers. Others prefer more conservative strategies, choosing to minimize losses even if this means sacrificing potential profits. This variability in risk responses reflects how each person handles uncertainty and pressure.

Emotions also play a crucial role in the psychology of the trader. From euphoria when our trades go well to fear and anxiety when the market turns against us, our emotions can have a profound impact on our financial decisions. The key to managing emotions is not to suppress them, but to learn to recognize and manage them effectively so as not to let them dominate our decisions.

Another fundamental aspect of the trader's psychology is the attitude towards losses. In the world of trading, losses are inevitable, but how we face and interpret them can make the difference between success and failure in the long term. Some traders may become demoralized by a loss and abandon their strategy, while others view each loss as a learning opportunity to adjust and improve their approach.

In this chapter we will explore in depth how understanding and managing your own psychology as a trader can be the key to improving your performance and making more informed decisions. You will discover practical techniques to develop a resilient mindset in the face of market volatility, effective strategies to manage stress, and how to create an emotionally healthy environment to boost your trading performance.

Get ready to immerse yourself in the fascinating world of the trader's mind and discover how you can use this understanding to take control of your financial operations!

The Impact of Emotions on Trading Decisions

Imagine that you are in front of your computer, ready to make a trade in the market. At that point, your heart is beating a little faster than normal because the price is rising rapidly. You may feel a mix of excitement and nervousness. Should you enter the trade now or wait a little longer?

Emotions play a crucial role in every decision you make as a trader. When you're excited because the market is going in your favor, it's easy to be tempted to take more risks than usual. This could lead you to open more positions than you initially planned or to hold a trade longer than recommended, hoping for even greater profits.

On the other hand, when the market starts to move against you, fear and anxiety can take over. You may feel the urge to close the trade to avoid further losses, even if your original plan indicated otherwise. These types of emotional reactions can lead to impulsive decisions that go against your trading strategy.

It is important to recognize that we all experience these emotions, even the most experienced traders. The key is not to eliminate emotions (because that would be impossible), but to learn to manage them effectively. This involves developing an emotional awareness of how you feel in different market situations and how those emotions can influence your decisions.

In this chapter we will explore how emotions such as euphoria, fear, greed and regret can significantly impact your trading decisions. You will learn practical techniques for staying calm under pressure, strategies for making more objective decisions, and how to adjust your trading plan to mitigate the impact of emotions.

Understanding how emotions affect your decisions will give you an advantage in the market. By learning to manage your emotions and make more rational decisions, you will be on a better path to achieving your long-term financial goals as a trader. Get ready to explore how taking emotional control can make the difference between success and failure in the world of trading.

The Importance of Emotional Control

Imagine that you are in the middle of a trading session. The market has taken an unexpected turn and your emotions are in a whirlwind. Without adequate emotional control, you could make impulsive decisions that could put your profits or even your initial capital at risk. It's like being on an emotional roller coaster where every rise and fall of the market can trigger intense responses.

Emotional control in trading is like having a superpower. It allows you to remain calm and composed, even when the market is at its most volatile. This doesn't mean suppressing your emotions, but learning to recognize and manage them so they don't dictate your financial decisions.

When you have emotional control, you can follow your trading plan with discipline. This means not giving in to unbridled enthusiasm when things are going well, nor succumbing to panic when faced with losses. Instead, you can objectively evaluate each situation, make informed decisions, and adjust your strategy as necessary.

Additionally, emotional control helps you maintain a long-term mindset. You know that wins and losses are part of the game, and you don't let temporary setbacks discourage you. This allows you to stay on track toward your financial goals without getting distracted or derailed from your strategic path.

In this chapter we will explore why emotional control is essential for trading success. You will learn practical techniques to develop and strengthen your emotional control, from meditation and conscious breathing to emotional contingency planning. We'll also discuss how maintaining emotional balance can not only improve your financial results, but also your overall well-being.

Mastering emotional control is not something that happens overnight, but it is a skill that can be learned and perfected over time and consistent practice. Get ready to discover how emotional control can become your most powerful ally in the world of trading, helping you navigate the turbulent waters of the market with confidence and determination.

Identification of Emotions

Imagine that you are trading in the market and suddenly feel a wave of nervousness. What is really going on in your mind at that moment? Identifying your emotions while trading is like cracking a code that can influence your financial decisions.

Identifying emotions in trading involves being aware of how you feel in different market situations. It can be excitement when a trade goes in your favor, fear when the market moves against your expectations, or impatience when you wait for results. Recognizing these emotions is the first step to managing them effectively.

A useful technique for identifying emotions is introspection. Take a moment to reflect on how you feel before, during and after each operation. Are you excited, anxious, confident or worried? Writing down your emotions can help you spot patterns and understand what triggers specific emotional responses.

In addition to introspection, observing your behavioral patterns is also crucial. Do you make riskier decisions when you're excited by a winning streak? Are you more likely to avoid losses by closing trades too early when you feel afraid? Recognizing how your emotions influence your decisions will allow you to take steps to better manage them.

In this chapter we will explore practical techniques for identifying and labeling your emotions while trading. You will learn strategies to keep an emotional record, such as keeping a trading journal where you document your emotional states and the decisions you make. We will also discuss the importance of emotional self-awareness in improving your performance as a trader.

Identifying your emotions gives you a significant advantage in trading. Not only does it help you better understand your own drives and motivations, but it also allows you to make more informed and objective decisions. Get ready to discover how the ability to identify emotions can transform your approach in the market, taking you one step closer to achieving your financial goals.

Strategies to Reduce Emotional Influence

When it comes to trading, staying calm under pressure can make the difference between success and failure. Here I present some practical strategies to reduce emotional influence and improve your performance in the financial market.

One of the most effective strategies is to establish clear rules and follow a predefined trading plan. This helps you stay focused on specific goals and avoid making impulsive decisions based on momentary emotions. By having a well-structured plan, you reduce uncertainty and feel more confident in your decisions.

Another useful technique is to practice emotional self-awareness. This involves recognizing your emotions in the present moment and how they may be affecting your judgment. You can do this through meditation, conscious breathing, or simply taking a moment to evaluate how you feel before making any trading decisions.

Additionally, it is important to set clear limits for both profits and losses. This helps you manage risk effectively and prevent emotions from leading you to overexpose yourself in the market. Having limits allows you to operate in a more disciplined manner and protects you from impulsive decisions that could affect your capital.

Time management also plays a crucial role in reducing emotional influence. Setting specific times for trading and rest allows you to maintain a healthy balance between trading and other activities. This helps prevent emotional fatigue and keeps you focused and alert during trading sessions.

Finally, surrounding yourself with a community of traders or seeking the support of a mentor can be invaluable. Sharing experiences with other traders and receiving constructive feedback can help you gain perspective and maintain a positive mindset even during difficult market times.

In this chapter we explore these strategies and more, all designed to help you reduce emotional influence and improve your performance as a trader. By implementing these techniques, you will be better equipped to face the challenges of trading with confidence and emotional control. Get ready to transform your approach to the market and reach new levels of financial success!

Paige Beckham

Mindfulness and Trading

Imagine that you are trading in the market and suddenly you realize that your mind is wandering, worrying about what might happen if a trade doesn't go as you expected. Mindfulness in trading is like having a switch to return to the present and focus on what really matters: the decisions you are making at that moment.

Mindfulness is about being aware and present in the here and now, without judging or getting carried away by emotions from the past or worries about the future. In the context of trading, this means observing your thoughts and emotions while you trade, but without automatically reacting to them.

A key mindfulness technique is full attention to breathing. You can practice by simply taking a few moments to focus on your breathing: consciously inhaling and exhaling. This helps you calm your mind and reduce stress before, during and after trading sessions.

Another useful practice is the observation of thoughts. Instead of automatically identifying with every thought that arises (like "this is going to be a disaster" or "this is going to be great"), practice observing thoughts as clouds that come and go. This helps you maintain a healthy distance and make more objective decisions.

Mindfulness also helps you develop greater emotional self-awareness. By becoming more aware of how you feel in different trading situations, you can recognize early warning signs of intense emotions such as fear or euphoria. This allows you to respond more calmly and rationally instead of reacting impulsively.

In this chapter we explore how integrating mindfulness into your trading practice can improve your focus, reduce the influence of emotions and improve your decision making. You will learn practical techniques to cultivate mindfulness during trading sessions, as well as how to apply these principles to maintain a healthy emotional and mental balance in your trading career.

Get ready to discover how mindfulness can be a powerful tool to not only improve your trading performance, but also to enrich your overall quality of life. It's time to bring more calm and clarity to your financial operations!

Techniques of breathing and relaxation

Imagine that you are in front of your trading screen, feeling the pressure of the market and the emotions that arise. Breathing and relaxation techniques can be your secret allies to maintain calm and mental clarity in those intense moments.

A simple but powerful technique is diaphragmatic breathing. This involves breathing deeply from the diaphragm, rather than quick, shallow breaths from the chest. You can practice by placing one hand on your abdomen and making sure it rises and falls with each deep breath. This helps calm the nervous system and reduce immediate stress.

Another effective technique is square breathing or 4-7-8 breathing. It consists of inhaling for 4 seconds, holding your breath for 7 seconds and exhaling for 8 seconds. This breathing pattern helps balance the autonomic nervous system and promote deep relaxation in times of tension.

Mindfulness can also be applied to breathing. By focusing fully on each inhale and exhale, without judging or trying to change anything, you can train your mind to be present and focused. This practice not only calms the mind, but also helps you maintain attention during prolonged trading sessions.

In addition to conscious breathing, techniques such as progressive muscle relaxation are useful for releasing accumulated physical tension. It consists of tensing and then relaxing each muscle group, starting from the feet to the head. This not only relieves physical tension, but can also have a calming effect on the mind.

In this chapter we explore how these breathing and relaxation techniques can be practical tools to improve your emotional and mental well-being while trading in the financial market. You will learn how to integrate these practices into your daily trading routine to stay calm under pressure, reduce the impact of emotions, and make more informed and objective decisions.

Get ready to discover how the power of breathing and relaxation can transform your trading experience, providing you with powerful tools to navigate the ups and downs of the market with greater confidence and peace of mind. It's time to take a deep breath and operate calmly!

Developing an Emotionally Resilient Trading Plan

Imagine you are building a fortress, but instead of stones and mortar, you are building a trading plan that can withstand the emotional onslaught of the market. Developing an emotionally resilient trading plan is like having a detailed map that guides you through emotional storms and keeps you on course toward your financial goals.

The first step to developing a resilient trading plan is to set clear and realistic goals. This means defining what you want to achieve with your trading: whether it is generating additional income, achieving financial freedom or simply learning and improving as a trader. These goals act as the lighthouse that guides you in times of uncertainty.

Another crucial aspect is defining your trading strategy. This includes deciding what markets you will trade, what time frames you will use, and what technical indicators or fundamental analysis you will use to make decisions. Having a clear strategy helps you maintain focus and reduce the temptation to deviate from your plan due to momentary emotions.

In addition, it is important to establish specific rules for risk management. This includes determining how much you are willing to risk on each trade, where you will place your stop-loss orders, and how you will handle profits. These rules act as an emotional security cushion, protecting you from impulsive decisions that could put your capital at risk.

The emotional part of the trading plan is also crucial. This involves developing strategies to manage your emotions, such as practicing conscious breathing, using relaxation techniques, and being aware of your thoughts and emotions while trading. Emotional self-awareness allows you to identify and address emotional triggers before they affect your trading decisions.

In this chapter we explore how to combine these elements into a comprehensive and emotionally resilient trading plan. You will learn practical techniques to set effective goals, develop a solid trading strategy, establish clear risk management rules, and manage your emotions to stay calm under pressure.

By developing and following an emotionally resilient trading plan, you will not only be better prepared to face market challenges, but you will also be building a solid foundation to achieve your long-term financial goals. Get ready to strengthen your focus and emotional resilience in the exciting world of trading!

Paige Beckham

Maintain Discipline in Emotional Situations

Imagine that you are in the middle of a trading session and suddenly the market takes an unexpected turn. Emotions such as fear or euphoria can begin to cloud your judgment, but maintaining discipline in these situations is key to avoiding impulsive decisions that could put your profits at risk.

Trading discipline means following your trading plan despite the intense emotions you may experience. This includes adhering to the rules you have established for risk management, such as your position sizes and stop-loss levels, even when the market moves against your expectations.

An effective way to maintain discipline is to always remember the main objective of your trading. Whether it's generating consistent income, achieving specific financial goals, or simply learning and improving as a trader, being clear about your purpose helps you stay on track when emotions try to derail you.

Another important aspect is continuous self-assessment. Reflecting on your past decisions and how emotions may have influenced them allows you to learn and adjust your approach for future operations. Constructive self-criticism is a powerful tool to strengthen your discipline and improve your decision making.

Time management is also key to maintaining discipline. Setting specific times for trading and rest helps you avoid emotional exhaustion and maintain focus during trading sessions. This allows you to make more objective and rational decisions, even when facing stressful situations in the market.

In this chapter we explore how maintaining discipline in emotional situations can improve your performance as a trader. You will learn practical techniques to strengthen your self-discipline, such as establishing daily routines, practicing patience, and keeping a trading journal to record your emotions and decisions.

By cultivating discipline in trading, you will not only be protecting your capital and optimizing your performance, but also laying the foundation for constant and sustained growth in the financial market. Get ready to strengthen your discipline and confidently face the emotional challenges that trading can bring!

Paige Beckham

Learning from Emotional Losses

Imagine that you have experienced a significant loss in a trading operation. Emotions like frustration, sadness, or even anger can overwhelm you. But learning from these emotional losses is essential to grow and improve as a trader.

The first step in learning from emotional losses is to allow yourself to feel those emotions. It's natural to feel disappointed or angry after a loss, but it's important not to let these emotions cloud your judgment. Allow yourself to experience the emotions, but then channel them into an objective analysis of what went wrong.

A useful technique is to do a post-mortem review of the operation. This involves objectively analyzing what went wrong, what decisions you could have made differently, and what lessons you can learn for the future. Instead of blaming yourself or others, focus on identifying the specific mistakes that contributed to the loss.

Additionally, it is important to adjust your mental approach towards learning and continuous improvement. Instead of seeing losses as failures, focus on how they can be opportunities for growth. Each emotional loss can offer valuable lessons to help you adjust your strategy, improve your risk management, and strengthen your emotional discipline.

Another strategy is to keep a trading journal where you record not only your trades and results, but also your emotions and thoughts during each trade. This allows you to track emotional patterns and identify triggers that may affect your decision making. Emotional self-awareness is key to avoiding similar mistakes in the future.

In this chapter we explore how learning from emotional losses can be a crucial part of your development as a trader. You will learn practical techniques for managing negative emotions, how to do a constructive review of losses, and how to use each experience to strengthen your trading skill and confidence.

By learning and growing from emotional losses, you will not only improve your performance in the financial market, but you will also develop a resilient and adaptable mindset that will serve you well throughout your trading career. Get ready to turn every emotional challenge into an opportunity for learning and growth!

Mentoring and Psychological Support in Trading

Imagine having someone by your side who not only understands the market, but also your emotions and challenges as a trader. Mentoring and psychological support in trading can make the difference between fighting the market waves alone and successfully navigating towards your financial goals.

Trading mentoring is like having an experienced guide who shares their knowledge, strategies and experiences with you. A mentor can offer you invaluable insight into the market, help you avoid common mistakes, and accelerate your learning curve. Additionally, a good mentor can also provide you with emotional support, understanding the emotional ups and downs you experience as a trader.

Psychological support in trading focuses on managing emotions and maintaining a positive and resilient mindset. This may include techniques for managing stress, maintaining emotional discipline, and strengthening self-confidence. A trading psychologist can help you identify and address emotional patterns that could be affecting your performance in the market.

One of the greatest advantages of mentoring and psychological support is accountability. Having someone to discuss your operations and decisions with forces you to maintain discipline and transparency in your approach. Additionally, receiving constructive feedback allows you to adjust your strategy and continually improve as a trader.

In addition to personalized mentoring, you can also benefit from trading communities where you can share experiences, ideas and receive mutual support. These communities offer a space to learn from each other, find inspiration, and stay motivated even in difficult times.

In this chapter we explore how mentoring and psychological support can enhance your development as a trader. You will learn about the importance of having a mentor, how to find the right one for you, and what benefits it can bring you. We will also discuss the importance of emotional support and how you can integrate psychological strategies into your trading routine to improve your well-being and performance.

By taking advantage of mentoring and psychological support in trading, you will not only be improving your technical and emotional skills, but you will also be building a support network that will accompany you every step of your trading journey. Get ready to learn, grow and prosper with the help of mentors and psychological resources in the fascinating world of trading!

Paige Beckham

Strategies to Recover from Large Losses

Imagine that you have experienced a significant loss in the market. It may feel like the ground has been pulled from under your feet, but the truth is that all traders, even the most experienced ones, have been through tough times. The key is not in avoiding losses, but in how you recover and move forward.

1. Evaluate the situation without emotions: After a big loss, it's crucial to take a moment to objectively evaluate what went wrong. Avoid blaming yourself or others. Instead, analyze the factors that contributed to the loss, such as hasty decisions, lack of risk management, or unexpected changes in the market.

2. Learn from experience: Every loss is a lesson. Reflect on what you could have done differently and how you can adjust your strategy to avoid similar mistakes in the future. Keep a trading journal where you can record your trades, emotions and thoughts. This will help you identify patterns and improve your decision making.

3. Establish a recovery plan: After a significant loss, it's tempting to want to quickly recover what you lost. However, this can lead to impulsive decisions. Instead, develop a step-by-step recovery plan. Define realistic goals and establish a schedule to achieve them, focusing on consistency and discipline.

4. Manage your emotions: Big losses can trigger intense emotions such as fear, frustration or hopelessness. Practice breathing and relaxation techniques to stay calm. Talk to a mentor or trusted friend for emotional support. Keep a positive mindset and remember that every loss is an opportunity to learn and grow.

5. Diversify and manage risk: Review your risk management strategy. Make sure you don't overexpose yourself on a single trade and consider diversifying your investments to protect your capital. Learn how to use stop-loss orders effectively to limit losses and protect your profits.

6. Seek support and learning: Don't face losses alone. Seek support from a community of traders, a mentor or a trading psychologist. Share your experiences and learn from others. The exchange of ideas and constructive feedback can be essential to your emotional and financial recovery.

In conclusion, recovering from large trading losses requires patience, discipline and a positive approach towards learning and continuous improvement. It is not just about recovering what was lost, but about strengthening your ability to face future challenges with confidence and resilience. Get ready to transform losses into opportunities for growth and success in your trading career!

Paige Beckham

Emotional Simulation Exercises

Imagine that you are in a flight simulator but, instead of airplanes, you are training your emotions to face the ups and downs of trading. Emotional simulation exercises are like rehearsals for your mind and heart, preparing you to handle any situation the market can throw at you calmly and clearly.

One of the most effective exercises is guided visualization. Close your eyes and visualize a typical trading situation: perhaps a trade that starts to go wrong, or a losing streak. Imagine the emotions you might feel at that moment: fear, frustration, the temptation to act impulsively. Practice staying calm and making rational decisions in the midst of these simulated emotions.

Another exercise is role-playing. You can do this with a friend or mentor: one acts as a trader facing an emotionally challenging situation, while the other offers support and feedback. This helps you practice communicating your thoughts and feelings clearly and receive constructive advice to better manage emotions.

Writing can also be a powerful form of emotional simulation. Write about a past experience where you faced a big loss or a moment of euphoria in trading. Describe your thoughts, emotions, and actions in detail. This helps you reflect on how you could have handled the situation differently and prepare to face similar challenges in the future.

Additionally, you can use technological tools such as biofeedback apps that monitor your physiological responses (such as heart rate or brain activity) while you practice simulated trading situations. This gives you objective data about how you react under stress and helps you develop strategies to better manage emotions.

In this chapter we explore how emotional simulation exercises can strengthen your ability to manage emotions in trading. You will learn practical techniques for visualizing, role-playing, reflective writing, and using biofeedback technology to improve your emotional resilience. By integrating these exercises into your training routine, you will be better prepared to face the challenges of the market with confidence and calm.

Get ready to turn emotional simulation into a powerful tool to improve your performance as a trader and achieve your financial goals with greater consistency and emotional control. It's time to train your mind as much as you train your trading strategy!

Paige Beckham

Post-Trade Analysis from an Emotional Perspective

Imagine that each trading operation is like a chapter in an exciting novel, where you are the protagonist facing challenges and making crucial decisions. Post-trade analysis from an emotional perspective is like going back after each chapter to understand how emotions affected you and how you could improve in the next episodes of the financial market.

The first step in this analysis is to separate emotions from technical analysis. It's natural to feel intense emotions after a trade, whether it's euphoria over a big win or frustration over a loss. However, to learn from each trade, it is essential to objectify your decisions and actions. Examine the data, charts and technical signals that influenced your decision to enter and exit the market.

An effective technique is to keep a trading journal. Record not only the technical details of each trade, such as entry and exit price, position size and final result, but also your emotions and thoughts at that moment. Did you feel confident, anxious, indecisive? This record allows you to identify emotional patterns that could be affecting your decisions and adjust your approach accordingly.

Another key aspect of post-trade analysis is constructive self-criticism. Instead of blaming yourself or others for a loss or overly celebrating a gain, ask what you could have done differently. Evaluate whether you followed your trading plan, whether you adequately managed risk, and whether emotions influenced your decisions. This approach helps you learn from each experience and improve your ability to make more objective and consistent decisions in the future.

Additionally, it is important to celebrate your successes and learn from your mistakes without getting carried away by extreme emotions. Maintain a balanced mindset and focus on continuous learning. Discuss your trading with a mentor or trusted colleague who can offer a constructive outside perspective.

In this chapter we explore how post-trade analysis from an emotional perspective can be fundamental to your growth as a trader. You will learn how to separate emotions from technical analysis, maintain an effective trading journal, practice constructive self-criticism, and seek external feedback to improve your skills and results in the market.

By integrating this approach into your trading routine, you will be building a solid foundation for making more informed and consistent decisions. Prepare your mind to turn each trade into an opportunity for learning and improvement, and transform your experience in the financial market into a true novel of success and personal growth!

Paige Beckham

Community and Support among Traders

Imagine that you are part of a large family of traders, where each member shares experiences, ideas and mutual support in the exciting world of trading. Community and support among traders are like the pillars that hold up this dynamic world, offering not only technical knowledge, but also camaraderie and encouragement in times of both success and challenge.

One of the biggest advantages of belonging to a community of traders is the exchange of knowledge. Here, traders of all levels share strategies, techniques and market analysis. You can learn new ways to analyze charts, identify patterns, or interpret economic news. This diversity of perspectives enriches your own approach and helps you improve as a trader.

Emotional support is another crucial aspect of the trading community. Trading can be lonely and emotionally demanding, especially when you are facing significant losses or losing streaks. In a community, you can find emotional support from people who understand the ups and downs of trading. Sharing your experiences and challenges with other traders can relieve stress and give you a fresh perspective.

In addition to emotional support, a community of traders can also be a place for accountability. When you share your goals and objectives with other traders, you commit to maintaining discipline and transparency in your trading. This can motivate you to follow your trading plan and avoid impulsive decisions based on momentary emotions.

Continuing education is another key benefit of belonging to a trading community. Many communities host webinars, workshops or study groups where you can learn from experts and discuss topics relevant to your development as a trader. This continuous training keeps you up to date with the latest market trends and helps you adapt your strategy to economic and financial changes.

In this chapter we explore how community and support between traders can strengthen your trading career and success. You will learn about the importance of knowledge sharing, emotional support, accountability, and continuing education in a vibrant community. By joining a community of traders, you will not only expand your trading horizons, but you will also build meaningful relationships that can last a lifetime.

Get ready to immerse yourself in a network of passionate and dedicated traders, ready to share, learn and grow together on this exciting financial journey. Join the community and discover the power of support between traders to achieve your financial goals with confidence and determination!

Paige Beckham

Continuous Review and Adjustment of the Emotional Control Plan

Imagine that your emotional management plan is like a detailed map that guides you through the emotional storms of trading. However, as with any journey, sometimes you need to review and adjust your route to adapt to changing market conditions and your own emotional experiences.

The first step in continually reviewing and adjusting your emotional management plan is honest self-assessment. Reflect on your last operations and how you felt in each one. Did you stay calm in times of pressure? Did you make decisions based on analysis or did you let emotions dictate your actions? Identifying areas where you could have improved allows you to adjust your approach for future operations.

A key aspect of any emotional control plan is risk management. Review your loss limits and how you have applied them in the past. Have you followed your risk management rules consistently or have you made impulsive decisions? Adjusting your limits and risk management rules based on your experiences helps you protect your capital and maintain emotional stability during market ups and downs.

Another important point is the identification of emotional triggers. We all have factors that can trigger intense emotional responses, such as the fear of losing money or the euphoria of an unexpected gain. Reflect on what situations or events tend to affect your emotional state and develop strategies to manage these emotions constructively.

Periodically reviewing your plan also means learning from your mistakes. When you face a loss or an emotionally challenging situation, take it as an opportunity to evaluate what went wrong and how you could have reacted differently. Adjust your plan accordingly, incorporating new strategies to improve your emotional discipline and make more objective decisions in the future.

Finally, don't forget the importance of flexibility in your emotional control plan. The financial market is dynamic and can present unexpected surprises. Being willing to adjust your plan based on market conditions and your own experiences helps you stay adaptable and keep moving toward your financial goals.

In this chapter we explore how continually reviewing and adjusting your emotional control plan can strengthen your ability to manage emotions in trading. You will learn about honest self-assessment, risk management, identifying emotional triggers, learning from mistakes, and flexibility as key components of an effective plan. By implementing these adjustments, you will be building a solid foundation to improve your consistency and success in the exciting world of trading.

Get ready to fine-tune your emotional strategy, face challenges with confidence, and move toward a more stable and rewarding trading career. Adjust your plan and navigate the market emotions with determination and resilience!

Paige Beckham

Maintaining Emotional Balance in the Long Term

Imagine trading as an emotional marathon instead of a sprint. Maintaining long-term emotional balance is like training to endure and thrive throughout that marathon, not just surviving the ups and downs, but growing and improving with each step.

The first step is to establish a solid foundation of emotional self-knowledge. Know your emotional strengths and weaknesses, and how you react under pressure. This will help you identify and anticipate emotions that could affect your trading performance. Keep a trading journal where you can record not only your trades, but also your moods and thoughts before, during and after each trade.

Time management and adequate rest are also essential to maintain emotional balance in the long term. Trading can consume a lot of mental and emotional energy, so it is important to schedule regular breaks and disconnect from the markets from time to time. Maintain a healthy balance between your personal and professional life to avoid burnout and maintain a clear perspective.

Another essential aspect is continuing education and personal development. As markets evolve and economic conditions change, staying up-to-date with new strategies and techniques helps you adapt and maintain confidence in your ability to make informed decisions. Participate in webinars, workshops and read books related to trading and emotional management to continue growing as a trader.

Building a strong support network is also crucial. Connect with other traders, whether online or in person, to share experiences, ideas and strategies. The community can provide not only emotional support, but also valuable perspectives and constructive feedback that can help you stay on track and overcome long-term emotional obstacles.

Additionally, practice self-care and stress management techniques. This can include regular physical exercise, meditation, yoga, or any activity that helps you stay calm and mentally clear. Learn to recognize the signs of stress and anxiety, and develop effective strategies to mitigate these negative effects on your emotional well-being and trading performance.

In summary, maintaining long-term emotional balance in trading involves self-knowledge, time management, continuing education, building support networks, and self-care. By integrating these elements into your life as a trader, you will be better equipped to face market challenges with calm, confidence and resilience. Prepare your mind and heart for the long term, and transform your trading experience into an exciting and fulfilling career!

Paige Beckham

www.ingramcontent.com/pod-product-compliance
Lightning Source LLC
Chambersburg PA
CBHW071952210526
45479CB00003B/913